C000045471

BOLANIRAN DEJI - ADEYALE

"The life experience of a sickle cell disorder survivor"
A message of hope to any person living with any
form of disorder or disability.

I AM A LIVING TESTIMONY: A LIFE
EXPERIENCE OF A SICKLE CELL
DISORDER SURVIVOR
&
A MESSAGE OF HOPE TO
PERSONS LIVING WITH ANY
DISORDER OR DISABILITY

BY:
BOLANIRAN DEJI-ADEYALE

I AM A LIVING TESTIMONY

Amazon.com
www.hadarcreations.com
boosun2k@gmail.com
Cover Design: Hadar Creations
Publisher: Hadar Creations
Editors: Dunamis Adebayo
Adesoji Adeyemi
Tokunbo Akintola
ISBN: 9798707969782

Table of Contents

DEDICATION

This book is dedicated to people living with sickle cell disorder, especially sickle cell patients in Africa where access to efficient healthcare delivery is still a major challenge; to those who have succumbed to the disease; and to the Almighty God who has kept me alive and given me the grace to use the story of my life to offer hope and encouragement to sickle cell patients and their families.

ACKNOWLEDGEMENT

I acknowledge God for being the reason for my existence. I also acknowledge those whom God placed in my life strategically, and who have been there all the years: My parent Mr&Mrs F. O Osuntuyi (now of blessed memory)

My husband Mr Ayodeji Adeyale, for being a caring and loving husband

My siblings: Mrs 'Funke Noble, Mrs Lydia Akinwumi & Mr Kunle Osuntuyi My Aunty Mrs M. M Akinola

Dr 'Lolu Oshinowo & Dr 'Bode-Law

I appreciate everyone who has played a supporting role, even if I don't mention them in this book. Thank you!

CHAPTER 1

RATIONALE

When asked what my reason for telling this story is, I said I only want to inspire and encourage other people facing the same challenge – make them live life to the fullest with the people they love. Encourage them to love, laugh, play and share like they were as fit as a fiddle. There's a good that has come out of my experience with sickle-cell anaemia, and that's the privilege to counsel and be a muse of hope to children with the disorder. Nothing beats the joy of earning their parents' trust in this regard. Trust me.

So, I thought "why not write my experience, so I can reach a larger audience, and spread this hope?" Why not reach other Sickle Cell Warriors with this *one* message: the doctor's report doesn't define you. Rather, embracing God's word for your life is, of all things, most important. I am a living witness to this!

We are overcomers...we are warriors.... we are survivors!

"For I know the plans I have for you, declares the LORD plans to prosper you and not to harm you, plans to give you hope and a future" (Jeremiah 29:11).

Furthermore, sickle cell patients are not abnormal people, the illness is not a curse and it is wrong to believe that investing in a child with the disorder is a waste of financial resources. With access to quality care, the symptoms can be controlled, and disease complications managed such that sickle cell patients can live normally, even to old age. It is this positive message that I am so happy to share with my fellow survivors and the world: that they, too, can be all they want to be in life.

Finally, this book is driven by a deep sense of gratitude for life and is a call of hope to all Sickle Cell Warriors to take the life they have been given and make the most of it. For as long as there is breath in man, there is a bigger picture already painted, that in which there are no limitations to what can be achieved in between the doctor's visits and frightening episodes that leave you wishing you could do more.

Of course, the challenges exist. And, for people like us, our life is rife with them, but everything works out an awesome victory for us, by God himself. Come to think of it? Without these obstacles, we'll never discover our incredible ability to beat them, and come out dancing still? If God is by your side, you will beat any challenge.

CHAPTER 2

THE EARLY DAYS

I was about seven or eight years old when my bone ached for the first time. Before then, I was the normal healthy child; or so I thought. Occasionally, I'd contract malaria; get a headache, and then boils. I remember *kunleka'atan* what you were told to do whenever you had a boil: kneel before a rubbish dump. It was just one of the myths we grew up knowing in Yoruba land in the 70s and 80s. If you grew up in south-west Nigeria, I am sure you can relate; and it's funny how we couldn't connect the dots, as we would often have those painful boils appear on our knees. Of course, if you kneeled, the boil would burst from the pressure. Wouldn't it? We were not brought up to ask questions actually; but I must admit some of those myths were good material for the enrichment of social interaction.

So, back to my first bone pain experience. It started in my arms, and the first thought I had was "Oh dear! I must have slept on it". Then, I used Robb or any mentholated ointment. No way! It brought no relief. So, mum and dad decided it was time to see the doctor. First Family Hospital in Oke Ira. I remember the hospital vividly because I'd visit more than once eventually. A lot more than once.

I do not know what the doctor told my parents, but I remember we were told to return the following day. I was to be admitted and then given some medication. So, as instructed, we returned, and then I underwent a blood transfusion. The details are blurry now, but I remember not spending the night in the hospital I was discharged that day. In my little girl mind, I had believed that the pain of that process will not reoccur. I was wrong. It happened again, and more often too in the arms or legs. Sometimes, in both limbs at once and, frequently, in one. I would often breathe a sigh of relief when I had the pain in just one limb because it meant that I could play a little, at least. As for *those* pains, they were terrible. At some point, the ointments stopped providing the needed relief, and then I'd ask that a heavy object be placed on the pressure point as it would, somehow, provide temporal relief. See? I had already found a way to cope with the bone ache. I was not a smart child for nothing.

If you thought the ache slowed me down in any way, think again, because I was an active sometimes restless and talkative child. It did not matter that I had to let my spirit loose despite the episodes of pain that lasted three to four days at a time. Ok, maybe I could not let it loose as much as I wanted, but I did my best in making sure I got some playtime with family and friends too. Children do not know any better. If they can move a limb, they would play. It is that simple.

I could not love my schoolteachers more because it must have been a lot of work to keep me still. Sure, I had good grades: I never went below the third position in the class. However, and this is funny the end of term report summary would read "she is too restless" or she "she is talkative". Dad did not like those comments, and he would often scold me and give some strokes of the cane. He probably felt I could take the first position in class always if I were not restless.

My parents never allowed the 'sickness' as an excuse not to do house chores. You could say they did not understand how gravely ill I could become, neither did I. All the children had to do house chores on weekends especially. Some of us would scrub the floor, clean the bathroom and toilets, then tidy up our surroundings generally. It was often boring at first but before long we would be found giggling excitedly through it all and would even do more than was required of us.

My father had a farm near the house; and, sometimes on Saturdays, we worked there as well. We would weed the farm and help in planting corn, yam, cassava and vegetables. We needed a lot of water for those chores and, at the time, there were not too many boreholes. We'd have to queue up at any of the few available, and then make several trips in filling the drums at home, sniffling, giggling and chatting along the way and, sometimes, with our clothes soaked. I was never exempted from any of those duties and I am eternally grateful to my parents for that. To be honest, they'd probably have exempted me from those chores, had they known the gravity of my health condition early on. However, in hindsight, I am glad it turned out that way because let's face it those chores really helped in building my character and preparing me for adulthood. They helped in making us independent, self-reliant and dutiful.

One thing I need to mention in all of this is that no matter how many times I fell ill, I never missed a school exam. I don't know how it happened; but even if I fell ill just days to the exams, I would always be ready, alert and strong enough to write them on D-day. On top of that, I would always pass with flying colours too. In short, I never let those aches get the best of me. They seem to disappear in the light of the prospect of coming out on tops in my exams. To be honest, it was just God's grace and mercy, because others had the same condition and would miss classes and exams, not being able to cope. Mine was just as a result of God's grace and mercy, and nothing more.

CHAPTER 3

BOARDING SCHOOL

I gained admission into secondary school at the age of 11 in 1989. I got admitted to four different boarding schools simultaneously. St Helens Unity Sec. Sch. Ondo, Federal Govt Girls College (FGGC) Kazaure Jigawa, St Louis Grammar Sch. Ondo and Lagos State Model College. It later became obvious that my parents wanted me in a girls-only school. They wanted the best for us and, whatever decision they took seemed to be in our best interest. They analyzed each school to decide which was best from all the available options not just academically but spiritually too. FGGC Kazaure was not an option because of the distance from Lagos. I had picked FGGC Akure as first choice and FGC Odogbolu as the second choice but, back then, you were posted to any of the schools, and not necessarily the one you filled out in the form.

So, the great distance knocked off FGGC Kazaure, and Lagos State Model College is a mixed school, so that was ruled out as well. My parents, who were devout Catholics, naturally wanted St Louis Girls Grammar School, as it was being run by the Catholic Church, and they had a Reverend sister as the principal, but Sister Cecelia, of blessed memory, said she couldn't admit me and my cousin to the boarding house. The reason was that so many parents were asking for boarding slots, so she told my dad that one of us had to take the boarding option, while the other would be a day student. Since I still had the admission at St Helens, my dad accepted that my cousin is admitted at St Louis while I went for St Helens.

I had never left home before then, and it was a very strange feeling, but I didn't cry. If nothing at all, I remember I was a little excited to discover what was in it for me. In a new school, to make new friends and begin another academic journey. The memory of what happened during my one-term stay at St Helens is quite blurry. First-term came to an end and my parents came to pick me, and I couldn't even say goodbye to my new friends. It happened so fast, and I didn't know I would not be returning to that school. I had the bone pain crisis many times. Terrible pains as always but I pulled through as I had always done. One memory stands out though -- a funny incident that happened during a visiting day or so: I had eaten so much homemade food from different people, and, by nighttime, I had a terrible stomach upset. The stomach upset became so unbearable in the middle of the night that I needed to use the toilet. Back then, there were only pit toilets available in the school and they weren't so close to the hostel. Before I could get myself to the pit toilet, I had pooed on myself. In retrospect, I will seize this opportunity to thank my cousin Mrs Ronke Oluokun who, although was two years my senior in school, took good care of me. I can't remember all of what happened after then, but I remember she helped in washing the clothes I had on that night. I can't thank her enough.

My mum's elder sister Mrs Akinola, who worked with Federal Govt College Odogbolu, came visiting during the holiday. I think I was just recovering from another bout of bone pain crisis at the time she visited. I was quite lean. I have never really been chubby anyway, as I had always been a lean child who didn't like to eat much.

Aside from rice, I am not sure I liked any other meal. I hated beans and other moulded Nigerian delicacies like Eba and Amala, popularly called *swallow*. Dad would have none of that, and would, sometimes, spank me for not eating anything else apart from rice. I was a bit of brat in dealing with this actually: sometimes, I'd pretend to eat and, when dad wasn't looking, would throw each handful under the table to be retrieved and disposed of properly when he wasn't looking. Now that I am a mother, however, I understand perfectly what my parents did. They wanted me to add some weight and build my immune system. God bless them for that. But, I hardly ate, and you can only imagine what I looked like when my Aunty came visiting, having just recovered from an illness. Oh, she was moved to tears, on sighting me, and promised to do everything in her power to get me into FGC Odogbolu, so she could take care of me while in school. How she did it, we did not know but she came back a few days to resumption with my admission letter and materials for my school uniforms. She had gone shopping for me on her way home. My dear aunty is God-sent. My life history can never be complete without her input, and that of the entire Akinola family. God used them in ensuring my wellbeing in boarding school, and I am forever indebted to them. Nothing I do can ever measure up to the impact they had in my life, and I pray God reward them continually by sending the right people their way in their time of need too, Amen!

Our lives are in God's hands, he has them all planned and his plans for us are for good. My parents wanted me admitted to a girls-only school; but I spent a term only. I do not know if I would have survived had I remained at St Helen's School with the frequent illness. I am convinced that God made my admission to FGC Odogbolu possible so I could survive those crises and used my Aunty and her family greatly to achieve this.

CHAPTER 4

SICKLE CELL DISORDER DEMYSTIFIED

In April 1988, my parents lost their last child. He was only two and a half years old. I still remember vividly everything that happened that day and the events that led to his death. I remember seeing my mum's diary sometime later and, against that date, she wrote: "the straw that broke the camel's back". It was a depressing time for everyone, and that death must have hit my parents so much. No one prays to experience such in their lifetime, you can, therefore, understand the aftermath, and why my parents were ready to do anything to ensure they didn't lose another child. So, the medical and spiritual journey began.

As Nigerians, we tend to believe there is a spiritual undertone to everything. One of my aunt was a staff of the Ondo State Specialist Hospital, Ado Ekiti at the time, so my siblings and I visited in the long holiday for a proper medical checkup. I'll digress and narrate the funny stunt I pulled at the hospital. I have always hated the injections. I hate anything that has to do with hospitals. So, when we got to the hospital and got to know they'd be taking blood samples from us, I drew back and allowed my siblings to go first. When it was my turn, I ran away upon sighting the sharp needle. Dad was angry and scolded me for putting up such a show at first. The hospital staff had to pin me down to get the blood sample after a hot chase. In the end, the result revealed my blood genotype as SS. I had the Sickle Cell Disorder, and this was what triggered the bone pain crises of all those years; and for twelve years, my parents didn't know this.

Sickle cell disease is a genetic disorder that makes the blood produce abnormal red blood cells known as sickle cells. Red blood cells are round, and the shape allows them to move with ease throughout the body, but a person with SCD has some of the cells curved like a sickle. These sickle-shaped cells don't flow easily through the blood vessels and can even get stuck. When these cells get stuck, they slow or completely block blood flow. This development leads to a sickle cell crisis. Since they hinder blood flow, it means some parts of the body are starved of oxygen and this, therefore, leads to acute and chronic pain which can last from a few hours to even weeks. The pain is often felt in the chest, belly, arms and legs. A person gets the disease when they inherit a sickle cell gene from each of the parents.

Clearly, for the first twelve years of my life, my parents didn't know I had sickle cell disorder. At a time when there was an almost complete lack of awareness of SCD, it is very likely many young children born with the disease died without receiving proper medical care simply because their ailment wasn't accurately diagnosed. It is also worth mentioning that many children of my age, or younger at the time, died because most parents probably thought they were *ogbanje:* a superstitious belief that children who fell ill too often were affected by the marine spirit. I think I must have been fortunate, especially, that dad did not equate my refusal to eat Amala and Eba with the *ogbanje*. Thank goodness he knew better!

Despite the shocking revelation, my parents still decided to seek spiritual help. As Christians, we believe in the power of prayers and we got a lot of referrals to churches where the pastors were said to be powerful and I could be healed. We visited different churches, and it was during one of those visits that we were at a white garment church somewhere in my hometown. The *Woli* (Prophet)said I was an *Eda*. I don't even know what that means in English, except that it loosely translates to "unusual creature". He also mentioned that it was my *Egbe* (spiritual group members) who wanted me back home in the spirit world. Laughable. Oh yes, my parents went with the flow. Understandably so, because they were now at their wits' end, so to speak. *Woli* said I needed 'deliverance', so the *Egbe* could let me be fine.

On the said day of 'deliverance', I was taken to a stream; stripped naked and thrown into the river. My most prized possession then, my gold earring with blue stones (it was a gift from my mum for my tenth birthday) was also taken off and thrown into the river. Oh, how I cried! I loved that pair of earrings so much but that was not all: *Woli* also brought out a broom and beat me with it several times, all in the name of deliverance saying all sorts with each stroke, and thinking that my sharp cry of pain, was a sign that the *Egbe* were releasing their hold on me for good. Then, after the punishment of course, he told my mum to bathe me in the river with the special sponge upon which he had 'prayed'. Now, imagine having me, in that state, having a bath in the river, in the cold harmattan. Add to that the stinging pain from the beating. My parents, in their desperation to have me healed, didn't know any better than to comply with *Woli's* directives. Unfortunately, all of the theatrics did nothing to stop the bone pain and illness. They became more frequent and even worse after *Woli's* 'deliverance'.

GOD'S FAITHFULNESS

I pray you will not be tempted beyond what you can bear. Losing a child is a great pain. I have been there and, as much as you can, you will do anything within your power to ensure it does not happen again. However, God is ever faithful; His mercy endures forever. His mercy kept me. His banner over me is love. I give him all the glory, the entire honour and all adoration. I remember I used to ask God at the time: "why me?", and the answer was always clear: "I am with you". One thing is clear; God never leaves nor forsakes His own.

Like the man who was born blind in the Bible in John 9:1-12, of whom Jesus asked in testing his disciples if it was a result of his sins or those of his parents. Jesus replied: "Neither this man nor his parents sinned but this happened so that the works of God might be displayed in him." This is my testimony: the works of God are being displayed in my life daily. After the diagnosis, I was told to avoid anything cold. That meant I had to stop drinking cold water and stop bathing with cold water. As of today, I still keep to the "don't bath with cold water" part of the doctor's advice but the "not drinking cold water" part is almost impossible for me. Ah! Drinking ordinary water is boring *jare.*

I was also placed on daily medications. The truth is: I was faithful with the regimen in pregnancy only. It's not that easy to stick to your regimen religiously. Trust me, I know this. My parents bought them regularly. When I was going to the boarding house, and at every resumption, my dad would buy lots of them because he didn't want me to run out of them while in school. Stubborn me; I wouldn't even touch those drugs, and would save them in the box until the end of the school term, only to throw them in the trash. I just hated those drugs, and still wonder how on earth I survived without them in boarding school with the stress that comes with hard study, play and even the occasional illness. It's one reason I know God was just merciful.

Folic acid, for instance, was supposed to prevent my blood level from going down, but I never took it. I had acute pain crises, but miraculously my blood level never went down. Each time my dad took me to do a packed cell volume (PCV) test, the result was always 30. The doctors always told my dad that I must be lucky. Later in life, I realized it wasn't luck, but God's mercy. Of course, Dad never knew I didn't take the medicine; he probably assumed they were the ones helping my PCV. I recall that my grandmother and other well-wishers brought different kinds of local herbs too.

Grandma. Bless her soul! She'd bring local herbs *Agbo.* Bitter as anything. Of course, they went the way of the tablets too. If I couldn't stomach tablets, how do you expect me to drink those herbs? To the trash, they went. Grandma's *Orinata* wasn't as bad, maybe. It was a special chewing stick I was meant to chew for a while, then swallow the sputum extract. Alas, *Orinata* went to the trash too. Sorry.

CHAPTER 5

BOARDING SCHOOL

Malaria lowers the blood volume and I often contracted it in boarding house. Back then, the large expanse of land that was FGC Odogbolu was mostly undeveloped, so there were lots of mosquitos. Each student was expected to use a mosquito net, but I didn't like it much. Every time I tried to sleep under a net, I felt choked-- like I was going to suffocate to death. So, like the medications, I never used it; and, you guessed right, malaria *showed me pepper.*

With constant malaria, came the sickle cell crises as well since my immune system was compromised even further. I remember being rushed to the dispensary or my aunt's house on many occasions for the needed care. Before long, however, I'd be back talking, playing and, of course, refusing to take my drugs or use the mosquito net. All I wanted was to be like every normal kid. I guess my spirit was too alive for this flesh. It still is and is the reason I am undeterred.

I was not used to the cold-water bath and getting hot water in the hostel wasn't possible. So, my Aunt advised "rub and shine" before classes. Anyone who went to boarding school would know "rub and shine": wake up, and then moisturize your skin without having a bath, then dress up, and you are off to school. Better still, you could have a bath the night before when it was a lot warmer and you need not bathe in the morning. The boarding school life was known more for its many improvisations and "rub and shine" was my favourite. However, after classes, I'd go to the school kitchen to get some hot water, so I could have a proper bath. It was a good thing that my aunt was the Senior Catering Officer in charge of the kitchen. So, the kitchen staff knew me and would make hot water available in the afternoon, whether my aunt was there or not. God bless them all, wherever they are now.

There was a staff block for one housemistress to reside in the girl's hostel, and when we resumed the session for JS2, Miss Mahmud (now Mrs Arikewuyo) was appointed to move into the teachers' quarters in the girl's hostel. She saw me bringing in water from the kitchen one of those afternoons and inquired what I wanted to use if for. She then went to see my aunty and told her, henceforth, she would make hot water available for me every morning. That was how I started bathing in the morning again. God bless her wherever she is too. Mrs Arikewuyo ensured I always had hot water available every morning from JS2 until I left 'Fego'Odogbolu. My parents always ensured they thanked her every time they came visiting. She was another God-sent.

I never liked the idea of having to wait until the afternoon to have a bath. Sometimes, Mrs Arikewuyo would make the water hot, and other girls in the hostel looked forward to mixing their water with mine, so they could also have a hot water bath, as Odogbolu was an extremely cold town, especially during harmattan. Anytime I came to Odogbolu, after I left secondary school, I always made sure I went back to thank Mrs Arikewuyo for what she did for me at the time. I could never repay all these people enough even if I attempted to and I wish to be in touch with them again. Mrs Arikewuyo would later be transferred to one of the FGCs in Kwara State and there were no mobile phones to keep in touch with her at the time.

I did mention that I didn't let the sickle cell disorder deter me. I remember joining the Man O' War (a para-military social group open to students) inJS 2 and, in hindsight, I laugh at myself. What was I thinking? Aside from the fact that I was ridiculously small and skinny in stature, Man O' War was rigorous. We were made to roll in the dirt, yell and jog. It freaked my aunt and her husband out. Guess what; I didn't leave the group. However, I didn't do much in the Man O' War except match past during the inter-house sports competitions, but I enjoyed the displays and the war chants that we made during rehearsals. I screamed myself hoarse and relived every moment of it one of the moments I am glad I savoured. I think I was in the Man O' War only until the end of JS 3.

In all, my secondary school days were fun; and the fact that mine was in a boarding house made it even more fun. Oh yes, you could say junior students didn't have as much fun as senior students because they were always at the receiving end of harsh treatments by bullish senior colleagues. However, in hindsight, nearly everyone who went to boarding school would say even that was part of the fun experience in the end.

Aside from my very playful tendencies despite SCD, the late onset of puberty made me look the part a lot more. Breast development didn't start until I was 16 years, menstruation also didn't start until

16 years too after I had left secondary school. Some of the boys in my set would make fun of that. "Breastless" they'd call me and would sometimes make a list of the "breastless girls" in school. Of course, I'd find my name on it. Those brats! Yes, they taught me to develop a thick skin to their juvenile jabs. We were all just kids, really, and rarely gave thought to the possible effect of our actions or words. What about me? The few times I'd take advantage of my frequent illness in courting favour from my friends. I won't lie, I enjoyed those moments of indulgence too.

On my last day in FGC Odogbolu in 1994, My dad came to pick me and my siblings. The usual practice was to go to the Akinola's house (my Aunty) in the staff quarters before heading to Lagos. My Aunty started a praise and worship session before we left. She was indeed very grateful to God that despite all the crisis I had, I survived and was able to complete my secondary school education. She narrated a testimony that happened once when I had a terrible crises and students had rushed to her house to call her and I was in terrible pains that didn't look like I would survive. She had stayed up all night praying for me. She fell asleep shortly after the prayers and had a dream. She said that in the dream, she saw Baba Obadare laying hands on me and praying for me. By the time she woke up, she started to give God thanks for answered prayers. She said after that day, my crisis greatly reduced and became almost nonexistence.

CHAPTER 6

MY UNIVERSITY DAYS

I got admitted to UNIBEN in 1997. I had completed an OND programme in 1996, started my industrial attachment immediately, and was looking forward to going back for HND when my dad insisted I complemented my qualification with a university education.

Dad worked in an organization where there was real discrimination against the HND qualification in favour of the BSc; so nothing I said about going back for an HND programme was accepted by him.

At the time I attempted, admission exercises were almost concluded in many universities and I told my dad I'd lose a year if I had to wait until the following year before getting a direct entry to the university. For my dad, that was no issue, as what was important to him was that I wasn't going back for HND. As God had it, the direct entry form for the 1996/1997 session was still on for sale, even though the admission exercise was rounding up in many schools. I bought the form, completed it and submitted quickly. By this time, the first and second batch lists were already concluded at the University of Benin.

My dad leveraged his relationship with the then VC of UNIBEN, in trying to secure an admission. As for me, I had given up, not thinking my application would scale through since it was done late. However, as Scripture says: God has plans for us and they are always good. My name didn't show up in the third batch and I thought my dad would give it a rest. From what we heard, the third batch was always the last list in UNIBEN before the start of the session; but, that year, there was a supplementary list and, guess what, I found my name on it. The list came out on the day of matriculation! As a direct entry candidate, I was admitted in Year Two and, by the time I joined, the session was well underway, and I had a lot of catching up to do. This was what fuelled my determination to stay focused on my academic work and keep playtime or social interaction to the barest minimum. Back in the OND days, I had been strongly involved in the Catholic Charismatic Renewal Fellowship and was an executive member of the Catholic Students Association. Now, I knew I couldn't take up such responsibility; not with so much catching up to do in UNIBEN. After some weeks, I asked a family friend, with whom I squatted, if there was a Catholic Charismatic Renewal Fellowship on campus. She mentioned that there was one, but she wouldn't advise me to join them. Anyway, I decided to see things for myself –you know, I was a bit stubborn –so I decided to check out the fellowship. Girl! I fell in love with the fellowship right away!

CHAPTER 7

MEETING CHRIST THE SAVIOUR

My story is incomplete without mentioning the fellowship (Light of Christ Community, Catholic Charismatic Renewal). It was at the fellowship that I met Jesus Christ. The undiluted word of God was being preached and I experienced genuine love. From my very first day at the fellowship, I knew there was no going back. Even when the fellowship had issues with the main church and many members left, I knew it was God who ordered my steps there and I couldn't be convinced to leave. No one knew my health status. I still had sickle cell crisis but I kept it to myself. For me at that time, SCD was shameful; persons with SCD were often discriminated against as a result of little or no knowledge about it and I felt people wouldn't want to associate with me if they knew my health status. Sometime in my third year (300 level), the president of one of the campus fellowships passed away. I learnt he died of SCD. I became so scared. If a fellowship president could die of SCD , what would be the fate of a babe in Christ like me? The information out there in the 1990s was that a sickle cell patient couldn't live beyond 21 years and I was 20 when this sad event happened. I felt as if my time to die was near.

I wrote a letter to the General Coordinator of my fellowship, telling him of my issues. It was he, GC Usi Oboh, who told me about Jesus the Healer, Jesus who could take away my pain, Jesus the balm in Gilead. He assured me that because someone died, didn't mean I will. He told me to search the scriptures for all Bible verses on healing, divine health and long life. That was how Isaiah 53: 3-5, Romans 8: 11, 1 Peter 2:24 and Matthew 8: 17 became my daily doses. I confessed them daily. Then, there was a leadership training program in the fellowship and Brother Rasheed Aruna, a past leader in the fellowship, who had graduated years before I came into UNIBEN, was invited to speak.

After Brother Rasheed had preached, he started to pray for everyone, one after the other. When it was my turn, he prayed for me and asked that I stepped aside. When he was done praying for everyone, he prayed for me again, like he knew what I was going through. That day became the turning point of my life. I knew I was healed and my deliverance had come. The crisis disappeared and I could stay a whole year without a single crisis. After then, the only crisis I had was in the final year and the pains didn't even last a day. After then, I had crises twice during NYSC. I remember the last one was during the Rural Rugged Evangelism organized by NCCF.

We had visited a village after Auchi (I can't remember the name specifically). NCCF/ Rural Rugged was the best part of NYSC. I loved preaching the gospel in those villages. It was Rural Rugged that made me fall in love with missions and volunteering with NGOs. During Rural Rugged, we would sleep in the classrooms of the school in whatever village we went to. The classrooms were mainly without windows, so it was always extremely cold and mosquitoes feasted on us. Nonetheless, we were thrilled by the experience and truly happy that we could make the sacrifice for the Gospel. It was during one of those times that I had another crisis. I still remember that day very well.

The terrible pains started at night, and there was nowhere in sight from which we could get medications. We only had paracetamol in hand. It felt like I wouldn't survive the night but, by the grace of God -- not only did I survive the night – the pains were gone by the following evening, and I was totally fine, again!

My dad later got me redeployed to Lagos after spending six months in Edo state. I remember being told by a friend during the NYSC orientation camp that I could be redeployed to Lagos on medical grounds and I wondered why would I want that. As far as I was concerned, the real fun of NYSC was in serving outside Lagos, and I met very lovely people during my stay inAgbede/Auchi. I didn't like the idea of being redeployed to Lagos. I met lovely people during NYSC in Lagos, but both experiences just couldn't be compared. All in all, I cannot thank God enough for sending me to UNIBEN and, most importantly, for ordering my steps to Light of Christ community(LCC). I have never seen a fellowship where so much love existed, and where love is so real and practical. I am still, and will always be, a part of the alumni fellowship, LOCCAF (Light of Christ Community Alumni fellowship). God ordered my steps to LCC, and that's why I can share my testimonies today. With the way I resisted going to UNIBEN, I know that my life is really in God's hands and his plans for me are plans of good. He is indeed a faithful God, Agbanilagbatan, Oyigiyigi, Oba Alewilese, Oba Aseyiowun, Oba Aleselewi, Oba Awibesebe. To him be all the glory and adoration.

CHAPTER 8

WORK BEGINS

I started work in one of the leading banks in Nigeria, shortly after completing the National Youth Service. I remember we were asked to go for medical screening, and one of the lies the devil told me was that the bank would reject me once the result revealed my condition. So, I was scared as I went for the test, but remembered that the God who got me the job was faithful to keep it; and to His glory, I still got the job.

Working in the Nigerian banking industry is especially stressful, but I have been able to cope well. I was writing the Institute of Chartered Accountants of Nigeria (ICAN) exams at the time, so I'd attend lectures after work and on weekends too. Amazingly, not once did I fall ill. That was until sometime in 2003 when I was moved to Cash and Tellering. I hated that function and, to make matters worse, there was a giant air conditioner behind our sitting area. I told the Head, Cash Services that the air conditioner wasn't doing me any good, but she said it was meant for customers and couldn't be switched off or regulated to a higher temperature.

Then, I started to fall ill to the extent of being admitted to the hospital. I'd get well and resume work only to fall ill again. I asked to be moved from Cash and Tellering, but the request was declined. In fairness to them, no one in the office was aware I had any medical issues. So, they saw no reason my job function should be changed. At this time, I was still writing the ICAN exams, so the stress of work combined with that of preparing for ICAN exams as well as the amount of cold I was being exposed to daily, took their toll on me. In fact, during this period, I contracted a bone infection. I had gone to the hospital many times and all the pain reliever they gave only worked for a few hours after which the pain would return worse. When the pain wouldn't subside, my dad called a doctor friend of his who worked in LUTH. He was the person who introduced us to a haematologist.

A haematologist is a medical doctor who treats patients with blood disorders and malignancies, including conditions such as leukaemia, lymphoma and sickle-cell anaemia. It was my first ever encounter with one, and she was the first person to give me a lecture on sickle-cell disorder and what kind of lifestyle I should adopt to manage the condition. There was no internet at the time, from which one could get information; and the doctors I had seen previously were general practitioners.

So, I was treated for the bone infection and that was the end of any form of crisis. Before I resumed work, my dad had gone to see my branch manager and explained to her why I needed to be moved from my job function. It was how I was redeployed from Cash and Tellering at last! Aside from the health issue, I was also happy to be redeployed from the Cash and Tellering job. It was at this time that I met a doctor. He was a customer of the bank and had come to do some transactions. I can't remember what led to the conversation, but I remember he was the first person that told me never to be ashamed of my genotype. He made me understand that it wasn't my fault or my making. That doctor was to be of great help to me several years after as I could call him anytime to seek for advice on any medical issue.

Like I said earlier, that was the last time I had a crisis. I did not adhere to the regimen because I hate drugs. I can't say I was exercising my faith; the truth is that I hate any form of medication and since I was no longer falling ill, there was just no reason to take them. I know it was God's mercy that kept me. Many times, I wonder why He is so faithful to me, even when I have been unfaithful many times over. Yes, the bible says: "He has mercy on whom He chooses to have mercy on" and that is exactly my experiences all these years.

CHAPTER 9

MY PREGNANCY EXPERIENCE

I got married in January 2008 and got pregnant in the same month. Everyone said it was better to register in a government hospital, but I didn't like the way government hospitals treated people. Nevertheless, I registered at the Lagos State University Teaching Hospital, Ikeja also known as Ayinke House, and then at another private hospital. I used both hospitals for antenatal care. I was considered "high risk" because of my genotype, so I was scheduled for antenatal care weekly from the twelfth week of the pregnancy.

All went well, including the pregnancy, until the consultants at Ayinke House felt my baby was not growing because my tummy refused to bulge. He sent me for a scan within the hospital and to another standard laboratory outside the hospital. Both results showed that my baby was fine and growing, but this man was just not satisfied. I was about 37 weeks gone at this time, and he decided to place me on admission, to observe me for a week. Even though I was in a private ward and used a mosquito net, I was bitten so much by mosquitoes that, by the time I was discharged, my PCV had dropped to 20. Before I became pregnant, my Packed Cell Volume was 30.

I was discharged on a Friday and my mum came visiting the day after that. I remember telling her that I didn't know what was wrong with me, but I knew I wasn't okay at all. My husband had gone out that morning to church. She called him and told him she was taking me to the private hospital where I had registered. We got to the hospital and I was placed on admission again. By Sunday, I observed that the baby had stopped kicking but because that was my first experience, I didn't think much of it. I just felt the baby wanted some quiet. By Monday morning, I told the doctor during his ward round that the baby wasn't kicking anymore. He did a scan immediately and said the baby was still breathing, but was distressed, so a caesarian section was to be conducted immediately. I was already 38 weeks gone at this time. That was around 10am on the 6th of October 2008. I called my hubby and my parents, and we prayed. Since it was an emergency CS, the hospital had to call for the anaesthetists as they did not have a resident one. However, the anaesthetist did not show up until 7pm. Her excuse for coming late. She had so many emergencies on her hands, among other excuses. As soon as the CS commenced, I was very nervous, so they gave me a little dose of sleeping injection. I wasn't deeply asleep and wasn't fully awake either. I finally woke up at the point I was being stitched up. The baby was brought out alive but her cry was very faint. All through that night, the hospital did everything to make her cry out loud, but she just gave only that faint cry. She was given to me to carry just once. I couldn't sit up to carry her well as I had just had a CS and was also having a blood transfusion. If only I knew that her survival was all that mattered. I later thought to myself that I should have tried to hold her longer. I have no regrets, but the experience will not be forgotten in a hurry.

CHAPTER 10

OLUWATOBILOBA

We named her Oluwatobiloba that night. The paediatrician was called upon but she couldn't come that night but came the next morning. I couldn't move around so I didn't know what was going on. By 5pm, it was obvious the hospital didn't know what to do anymore, so hubby and I decided to call the Medical Director of one of the big hospitals in Lagos, who was also a minister in the church we attended at the time. The man, immediately, ordered an ambulance to bring us to his hospital. I couldn't go with them, as I still couldn't move around. My husband went with the ambulance as Tobiloba was given all the care they could give, in transit to the new hospital. The medical report to the new hospital wrote that the APGA score was 4. Long and short of the story is that 'Tobiloba, my first and only girl passed on before the following morning, and my husband had to bury her.

No one told me what happened. My husband came to see me in the hospital the next day, Wednesday, and I remember asking him why he was not with 'Tobiloba. He told me, she was under intensive care and he wasn't allowed to stay with her. How I didn't suspect anything was wrong, I do not understand. My parents, hubby and all the hospital staff acted as if everything was fine. It wasn't until Friday night that I began to suspect something was wrong. I received a call from someone who said, *"Olorun o ni je ka riru e mo o"* (God will not let such happen again). I didn't get it at first and thought she was referring to the CS I just had. Before long, a nurse came to give me an injection that put me to sleep. I slept for so long and woke up almost noon on Saturday and I heard my mum call my dad that he should come. I was asking her what the issue was but she wouldn't say. My dad came in with the Reverend Father from his church. The doctor and nurses were also present in the company of a minister from our church along with his wife. By this time, of course, I knew something had gone wrong, but never did it cross my mind that 'Tobiloba' was gone.

The Reverend Father started a long sermon that didn't make any sense to me, the doctor took over from him and started telling stories that still didn't make sense. It wasn't after the lengthy talk that they broke the news, and it seemed like my world came crashing down. They wanted to give me another injection, but I refused it. I cried a lot. The minister from our church is the MD of the hospital where Tobiloba passed on. He told us that with the APGA score of 4 if she had survived, she would have grown to be a liability. So, even though it was a painful experience, we still needed to give God thanks. Giving God thanks at that time was the last thing on my mind. All I wanted was to be discharged from the hospital. It was a terrible time, but I took it in good faith. I was back in the hospital on admission by the next day in terrible pains, so there wasn't much time to even think about what happened.

The pain in my ribs and chest area was severe. I was admitted to the hospital, put on a drip, and given painkillers. The doctors understandably assumed it was another crisis and treated me with that in mind. However, the pain felt different this time around. Besides, I had not had a crisis in over five years. Somehow, I was convinced it wasn't a sickle cell crisis, but the doctor told me that a crisis could be in any part of the body, and not necessarily in the legs and hands as I had always thought.

The pain wouldn't subside, and I would be OK by morning. However, once it neared evening, I'd experience what felt like shortness in breath, and the pain would intensify all through the night. My mum stayed with me in the hospital all through the admission. The hospital staff would try to make me sleep with injections and drugs, but the pain wouldn't allow it. This continued for some days and I began to think it was a spiritual attack.

I remembered calling a close pastor friend, Pastor Kunle Adesanya, God bless him and his family, for being there for us to date. His type of person is rare. I told him that I was going to tell the hospital to discharge me since it was obvious, they couldn't handle the situation and that he should join his faith with ours as we prayed. So, I got discharged and went to my parents' house. I still needed my mum's care as I was still recovering from the CS delivery. By evening, I started feeling that I couldn't breathe again, the pain was back. I called my husband and pastor friend who prayed for me and believed God for healing; and God who had done it before did it again. I don't know how it happened, but the pain subsided until I was completely well without taking any medication. It was not until exactly a year later that I understood what God delivered me from. It was indeed a big deliverance and healing. All this happened in October 2008. I got well, went back home and resumed work. It wasn't an easy time. Thank God I had a very flat tummy so only a few people knew I was pregnant, and I didn't get too many questions about the baby, but the few people who knew would still say "congratulations, when were you delivered of your baby?". It was a trying time, but God saw us through.

CHAPTER 11

NEW PREGNANCY EXPERIENCE

By February 2009, I was pregnant again. It wasn't the best of time for someone who had a Caesarian Section just a few months ago. This coupled with my genotype. So, the stakes were higher now.

I wasn't taking chances, so I registered for antenatal care right from the start in the same private hospital I used the first time, even though everyone felt that I should have registered in a tertiary hospital. I got a letter from a colleague's mum to go to the military hospital. At this time, I had started spotting.

My hubby and I went to the hospital together and we met the military doctor. When I relayed the history of my pregnancy and told him that I was spotting, he advised I do another pregnancy test. I did the test, and it showed that I was pregnant; and then, upon showing it to the military doctor, he said that I couldn't register for antenatal care until I was 12 weeks gone because I was spotting. He even expressed his doubt that the pregnancy would stay. I wasn't too pleased with the bluntness with which he said it, to be honest, and then decided I wasn't going back to him.

After that visit, we decided to register at LUTH once I was 12 weeks gone. The spotting didn't stop; and it was so much on a particular day that the gynaecologist in the private hospital said he wasn't sure I was still pregnant – that I may have lost it – and, that he'd do a scan to confirm. It was the longest wait of life! My husband's head was bowed and I knew he was praying. I, on the other hand, couldn't bring myself to pray but cried instead. I was, by this time, overwhelmed. Thankfully, the scan showed that I was still pregnant, although I was placed on admission for a week, eventually, until the bleeding stopped. After that, I was discharged and then registered in LUTH as well, so I could have antenatal care in two hospitals. I wasn't going to take chances with this one.

Everything went well in LUTH until doctors threatened strike action. We had been told that we were going to have a planned Caesarian Section at 37 weeks, and this threat started when I was almost 33 weeks pregnant. I made my worries known at the office, and a colleague referred me to a hospital in Victoria Island, known for their top-notch gynaecological services. She told me it was a very expensive hospital, and that the office will not cover the cost, as they only used that hospital for senior management at the time. I told my husband about it and we decided to try them out. When I got to the said hospital and was told the cost of registration I almost turned back. I queried why I would pay so much for antenatal care but quickly recalled the last experience and realized money should be the least of my worries. So, I paid the fee.

The gynaecologist assessed my medical history, ordered a test, and gave me an appointment for the following week. I came in the following week as required and was told the doctor I saw the last time, was not on duty, so I was directed to see the Medical Director. When I was called in, the MD said he had gone through my file and was personally interested in my case. Interestingly, his first daughter had the sickle cell disorder, so he could relate with the situation. Therefore, he decided he was going to handle my case in person and carry out the Caesarian Section himself.

"Had you started antenatal care with us, we could have prevented this, but not to worry", the Medical Director added. He also told me that the medical bill could stack up to a million Naira, and he was aware that the company I worked for at the time wouldn't cover the bill.

"Nevertheless, I'd handle the matter and make them cover the cost", he said. He, however, informed me that they may not pay all of it, and I'd just have to pay the difference which wouldn't be too much for me, all the same. At this time, I was truly convinced that God was on my side. After this encounter, you can imagine what happened next. Of course,

I didn't bother going to LUTH or the other hospital.

Delivery was planned for 12th October. I came the day before and the nurses – to my amazement – said Baba (that is what they called the Medical Director) no longer performs the Caesarian Section surgery, and that they are sure he had told one of the other consultants to handle it. I wasn't bothered; I just wanted a safe delivery. The staff were all surprised to see Baba show up the following morning, all ready for the theatre.

Thankfully, I had a smooth delivery and, before 10am, my baby was brought out, after which I was moved to the recovery room for blood transfusion. We stayed in the hospital for five days and were given a bill of over N900,000. Baba called my husband and told him he had spoken with the Head of HR of the company where I worked, and we were to pay N190,000 only! I couldn't believe it. I'll say a little about Baba.

Baba isn't a Christian; neither is he a Muslim. He'd say he didn't believe God existed and only believed in humanity. Regardless, Baba let himself be used by God to save me. He is indeed God-sent. Baba wasn't only of great help for the delivery of my baby, but also in sorting the huge bill. He was also of great help to us for many years after that. Meeting Baba wasn't just a coincidence. God was in it from the beginning.

We christened the baby two days after I was discharged. The pain started that same day; just like what I experienced after giving birth to my first baby. It was terrible. I couldn't breathe, and then the pain would intensify suddenly, and I'd fear for my life.

I called a doctor friend (the one I met in 2003 who was a customer of the bank I worked for), immediately after the naming ceremony, who recommended a particular antibiotic medication that I was to use for seven days. The antibiotics helped a little.

I started postnatal care on the seventh day after delivery. The results showed that my baby was doing fine. I was asked to see the gynaecologist too. Baba wasn't on duty that day, as I would have preferred to see him instead, of course. I told him about the pain, and he asked me to do some tests as well as a chest X-ray. The results showed that I had pneumonia. Baba wouldn't let me return home, saying it was a good thing I took the antibiotics. However, he needed to observe me.

I told Baba that my baby was on exclusive breastfeeding, and he said: "you can only breastfeed when you are alive. Let your mum and husband take care of the baby". Pneumonia wasn't a sickness to be treated with kid's gloves especially with the level of pain I was in. I spent seven days in the hospital and, even after I left, Baba would check on me and ensure I got the best treatment. During that admission, my mind went back to the year before, when I had the same symptoms but was neither diagnosed nor treated properly. I could have died, but for God. I don't even know how to describe God's timely intervention, he saved, healed, kept and He did not abandon me from then to date. Even in my unfaithfulness, He is always there, and I acknowledge Him with a grateful heart.

CHAPTER 12

JOB LOSS

I gave birth to my son in October and was due to resume work in January. A week to Christmas as I got ready to resume work in two weeks the company decided to downsize. Unfortunately, I was among those relieved of their jobs. I was told that staff on maternity leave had been relieved of their jobs. I was devastated, to say the least, as it wasn't a good time at all. Nonetheless, I refused to wallow in self-pity. The next day, I started applying for jobs.

I remember being called for an interview immediately after the New Year's Day and not being able to attend with my baby, who was almost three-month-old at the time. My mum was yet to retire at the time but fortunately, my sister was on vacation, so she agreed to take care of my baby while I was away.

I couldn't breastfeed immediately I had my baby, so the hospital placed him on baby formula as soon as I was discharged; but I stopped the formula and breastfed him exclusively. So, I had to express breast milk in bottles before setting out for the interview. I also left the formula that we had opened at the time of his birth, in case I stayed out too long, not knowing it had spoiled. My sister didn't suspect anything until she noticed how it turned dark upon preparation. She decided to feed the baby with it, anyway, because she didn't think anything was wrong. Besides, the baby wailed endlessly. But for the unexpected visit of an older cousin who, immediately, raised the alarm, my sister would have fed it to the baby. It was how God saved us from another possible disaster. Our God is faithful. He watches over us.

CHAPTER 13

HIDDEN FIGURES

God often positions regular people, strategically, in life's journey to provide the most-needed solution, at certain crossroads. Often, these people won't always look like it at first.

I kept attending job interviews and, by March, I still hadn't gotten a job. Then one morning, I had the hunch to visit a former boss who worked in the Ikorodu branch of the bank, hoping to have his branch buy some of my husband's diesel and, better still, have him supply diesel on-demand as a contractor.

Unfortunately, the branch had a supplier already. While my former boss and I discussed, he called a friend at the head office, wanting to know if they had a job opening. He was asked to send my CV. This he did, immediately, as I made to leave for home. Before reaching home, I had gotten a text to attend an interview the following day. I honoured the invitation and was invited for a follow-up interview. It was the last I heard from the bank.

In April of that year, I got a job with a Lagos state agency. The salary was poor but, at that time, I didn't have a choice but to take the job. I was already settling down to the job when, at the end of June,

I got a call from the bank I applied to in March thanks, to my former boss. The caller introduced himself as the head of the department for which I was interviewed. He was impressed by my performance at the interview, he said, but wanted a staff that could be posted outside Lagos. I told him I just had a baby, and it would be difficult to relocate. He said there was nothing he could do as Lagos was full already. I contacted some friends working in the same department, and they advised I see him in the office, and not rely on a telephone conversation only. That way, we could have an honest conversation.

I was in the man's office the following day to tell him I needed the job and wouldn't mind being posted to Ogun state which is considerably closer to Lagos. In my presence, he called the Human Resources department and told them to re-add the name he had earlier instructed them to delete. That was how I got the job and resumed a few weeks later. Thank God I went to see him and thank God for the good advice from friends. Our God is indeed faithful. I have been on that Job from July 2010 to date and I would be ungrateful if I say God has not blessed me and my family in countless ways through it.

CHAPTER 14

ANOTHER PREGNANCY

About two years later, I became pregnant again. At the time, I was recovering from malaria. It also meant was that my blood level (PCV) was very low at the time. I, initially, registered at a private hospital near the house before heading to Baba in VI. By the time I got to Baba, he wasn't too happy. He felt I should have informed him when I wanted to get pregnant, so we could have planned it. Getting pregnant with a low Packed Cell Volume isn't good, he said. However, it was too late for all that, and he promised to ensure nothing went wrong. Baba said I was going to need a blood transfusion every 90 days. This was to prevent a crisis and to ensure that my genotype stays as AS almost all through the pregnancy since I was to be transfused with AA blood. He also said since I had two instances of pneumonia after delivery, he wasn't going to take chances. The plan was that I'd be given antibiotics in the last trimester.

The journey began. I saw Baba once a week and all went well. I also had the blood transfusion and started the antibiotics at the beginning of the third trimester. We knew we were going to have another Caesarian Section, so we chose 31st October for the operation. The pregnancy went on smoothly until the beginning of October when I started to feel strains in my rib area. It felt like something tugged at my rib. I also observed that the baby was no longer as active as usual, although he kicked well. After a week thereabout, I told my husband about the way I felt, and he advised I go to the hospital. I went to the private hospital near the house and I was given a chart with which I could track the number of times the baby kicked daily. Before the time, I would have recorded the tenth kick by 2pm. Now, it came at 4pm and, soon after, 6pm. That was when I knew something wasn't right. On my way from work that day, I went to the hospital near the house and told the gynaecologist what I observed. He did a scan immediately and said my baby was fine, but that I needed bed rest, so I could monitor the kicks in quiet. I went home but still felt uneasy, knowing something just wasn't right.

CHAPTER 15

MIRACLE BABY

I went to see Baba in Victoria Island the following morning and, as soon as he saw me at the gate, he asked: "Bola what is wrong with you?".

"I don't know", I said.

He immediately took me to a room with a cardiotocograph, a piece of equipment used in pregnancy to monitor fetal heart and contractions. A nurse was assigned to monitor the reading as well. I was to press the bell attached anytime the baby kicked. After about thirty minutes, the nurse called Baba to come and check the reading. After checking it, Baba declared, "It's like this your baby wants to come out o! Call your husband and tell him caesarean section will be done tomorrow."

I reminded Baba that it was October 17th, and the pregnancy was just 34 weeks. He replied, "Bola, something is wrong with your baby. I don't know what it is because the scan didn't show anything wrong." He added, "We can only help a baby when the baby is out if he remains in your tummy, a lot can go wrong. The worst that can happen is that he will need an incubator."

I called my husband to bring my hospital bag as the C-section was to be performed the next day. Fortunately, I had packed the baby things at 30weeks. Baba left and told the nurse to keep monitoring the reading. He came back again after thirty minutes and said the baby wouldn't wait until tomorrow; that we had to bring him out immediately. Worried, I called my husband, and told him to come down quickly, after which I called a few friends to pray along with us. Baba couldn't wait for my husband; so, he prepared me for an emergency C-section. They'd have to use what was available in the hospital for the baby. It was a good thing the hospital always envisaged such eventualities and would have made arrangements, just in case.

Unlike the last time when my husband was present and we conversed throughout the surgery, it was one of the doctors that talked with me this time.

By the time my husband arrived, I had delivered my second son through C-section. It was when he came out that everyone noticed that the umbilical cord was tightly wrapped around the baby's neck four times. The cord was also firmly wrapped around the legs. Baba, who said he didn't believe in God, remarked, "You truly must be serving a good God".

What if I hadn't come to the hospital that day? After all, the scan I did at the private hospital near our home showed the baby was fine. I just had the feeling that something was wrong. I thank God for Baba whom God brought my way. The cord was removed and he screamed his lungs out. The paediatrician, after examining him, declared that he didn't need the incubator. He weighed 1.95kg at birth. Although he was born with low birth weight, he had an Apgar score of 8. I was given a blood transfusion after the surgery.

I noticed that the hospital had improved its capacity to effectively manage patients' pain. This third caesarian section was the best because I felt no pain after it was performed. The pain was so well managed that by the next day, I was introduced to light meals. To the glory of God, we were discharged on the fifth day. The medical bill was over a million naira, but Baba gave us a discount, which brought it down to over nine hundred thousand Naira. We settled the bill without any issue. Baba named my son Owolabi because of the huge amount we had spent. My baby's naming went well, there was no pain (or pneumonia), and, unlike previous deliveries, I didn't have to go back to the hospital.

SUMMARY

Today, I still work for the Bank and I am involved in different foundations as a volunteer. I am currently the assistant coordinator of the Lagos zone of my alumni fellowship, LOCCAF and the Vice president of my set secondary school alumni (FEGO 94 set). I am also a member of the drama ministry of my church. I am living a very active life to the glory of God.

Living with a medical condition shouldn't stop us from achieving our purpose in life. It should even spur us on to succeed. I choose not to accept sickle cell disorder as a death sentence. I also refuse to believe being born with it means that God loves me less, or that He is unfaithful. I remember as a teenager, I always told myself that sickle cell couldn't kill me and couldn't stop me from achieving what I wanted to achieve. Some people assume, erroneously, that God is no longer God when they go through tough times. A sickle cell patient experiencing a crisis often has to deal with an existential crisis. Why did God create me this way? Is there even God at all? Does He care? How long do I have to continue to live with this pain? Life can be hard and unfair sometimes. And there is the element of suffering in human existence. As individuals, we are constantly confronted with different challenges. I guess one of mine is this disorder; but, I have kept the good fight.

We are aware that life is a struggle. We should therefore never resign to fate. I can't sufficiently explain how invaluable faith in God is. The Bible teaches us that when we go through trials and tribulations, we should put our trust in God for He gives us the power and the strength to overcome. Apostle Paul, when he was buffeted by "a thorn in the flesh," entreated God three times to take it away from him. God's reply was "My grace is sufficient for you, for My strength is made perfect in weakness" (2 Cor 12:9).

When asked by His disciples about why a man was born blind (John chapter 9), Jesus made it clear that the man wasn't born blind as a result of sin "but that the works of God should be revealed in him." God's glory is made known in our imperfections and weaknesses, provided we rely completely on Him for strength and protection. The Bible declares that God can make all grace abound towards us and that we can have sufficiency in all things. As I earlier pointed out, as human beings, we will have problems and challenges in life, and it is only good if we face them with courage and optimism. I strongly believe in being positive-minded. I live a healthy, normal life made possible by the grace and mercy of God. One thing I know, and I'm assured of is that my life is in God's hands. His thoughts towards me are thoughts of peace and His plans for me are good, they are to bring me to an expected end. I am continually emboldened by the scripture, "And we know that all things work together for good to those who love God, to those who are the called according to His purpose" (Rom 8:28).

To God be all the glory forever and ever. When I look at my life, several songs come to mind and I will like to share a few with you. These were some of the soul-lifting songs during those challenging periods and to date. Sing along!

SONGS:

1. *So, I am here today because God kept me.*

I'm alive today only because of His grace.
Oh, he kept me, God kept me, he kept me,
So, I wouldn't let go.

2. *Mo yin O logo o (2ce), ibi te sin mi de, me mo pe mo le de be o, Mo yin o logo o.*

3. *Just because of me, you gave up your life, at the cross of calvary, shedding your blood for me. What more can I do, what more can I say, than to praise you all my heart singing, Halleluia.*

4. *Melo ni moro, ninu ore ti Baba se. Me lo ni kin so, ninu ore ti Baba se. Ore re ma po, o ju iyanrin okun lo, me lo ni moro, afi kin sa ma dupe, ore re ma po, o ju iyanrin okun lo, melo nimoro, afi kin sama dupe.*

5. *O mu mi walaye, o seun o, o mu mi walaye, o seun o, Opo lo fe moo jo oni o, tikuti pa, aisan ti aye so pe ko to nkan, lo mu won lo. O mu mi walaye, e seun o.*

6. *E mi ni Jesu fe, O fe mi ye ye. E mi ni Jesu fe ran ju enikeni lo. O ra mi pa da l'owo Iku Ojiji o.*
   A yo I gbala lo wa di pu po repete.

7. *Great is thine faithfulness*

I AM A LIVING TESTIMONY

Oh Lord my father, there is no shadow of turning with thee

Thou changest not, thine compassion they fail not, as thou hath been, thou for ever will be

Chorus:

Great is thine faithfulness (2x)

Morning by morning new mercies I see,

All I have needed thine hands hath provided

Great is thine faithfulness

Lord unto me.

Summer and winter and spring time and harvest

Sun, moon, and stars in their courses above,

Join with all nature in manifold witness

To thy great faithfulness, mercy and love

Pardon for sin and a peace that endureth

Thy own dear presence to cheer and to guide

Strength for today and bright hope for tomorrow

Blessings all mine, with ten thousand beside...(chorus)

GLOSSARY

Èdá: An indigenous name for an unusual creature or being common with the Southwest(Yoruba) Nigeria

Egbé: Mischievous and spiritually co-opted alliance wit familiar or strange spirits

Jánjálá: A Southwestern Yoruba word which means tiny or remarkably small.

Kúnlèkátàn": A Yoruba expression meaning to the knee by the refuse dump. A detoxifying belief for boils.

'Ogbanje': A mystical belief that consistently sick children were affected and attracted by marine spirits.

Orin Ata: A local medicated chewing stick

Raison d'être: A French expression meaning 'reason' or 'rationale'

'Woli; A white garment prayer leader

ABOUT THE AUTHOR

Bolaniran Deji-Adeyale (FCA) holds a Bsc in Accounting, an MBA from Obafemi Awolowo University and is a Fellow of the institute of Chartered Accountant of Nigeria.

She had her secondary education at Federal government college Odogbolu, Ogun State.

She currently works for First Bank Nigeria Limited and has 19 years' experience in the Banking industry. Despite her remarkably busy working schedule, she has a passion for volunteering and has done this consistently for 10 years. Providing support for the less privileged in the society especially children and people living with sickle cell. She is a volunteer, fund raiser and financial donor to Crimsonbow Sickle cell initiative and Ask the Pediatrician foundation and is actively involved in their activities. Bolaniran is the first of three children born to the Late Mr and Mrs F O Osuntuyi.

She is married to Deji Adeyale and they are blessed with two Sons, Ayomide and Seyifunmi.

Printed in Great Britain
by Amazon

Help with HOMEWORK

ball

gloves

glasses

apple

television

socks

camping

cat

t-shirt

EASY ENGLISH
My Things
Vocabulary Book

books

dinner

dog

bed

clock

drink

AUTUMN
PUBLISHING

AUTUMN
PUBLISHING

Published in 2020
by Autumn Publishing
Cottage Farm
Sywell
NN6 0BJ
www.autumnpublishing.co.uk

Copyright © 2019 Autumn Publishing
Autumn is an imprint of Bonnier Books UK

0220 001
2 4 6 8 10 9 7 5 3 1
ISBN 978-1-83852-653-5

Written by Ben Ffrancon Davies
Illustrated by Sue Downing

Designed by Chris Stanley
Edited by Helen Catt

Printed and manufactured in China

EASY ENGLISH

My Things

Vocabulary Book

Introducing myself

My body

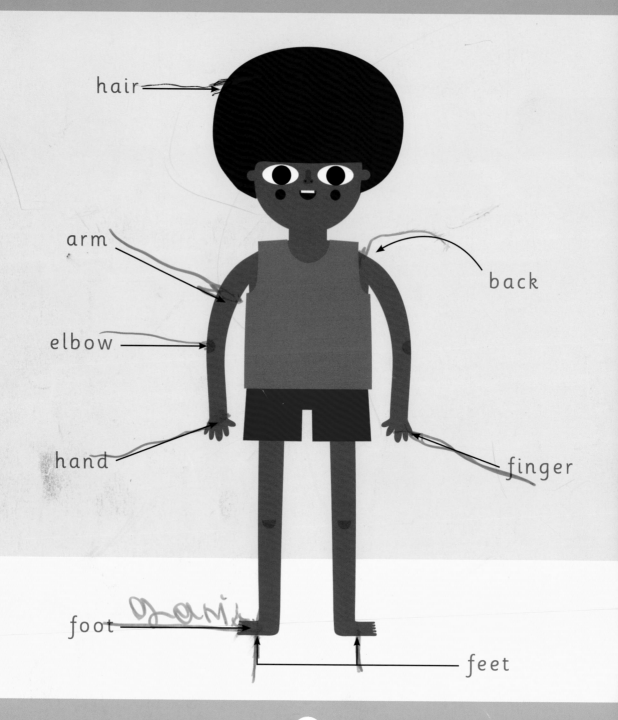

hair

arm

back

elbow

hand

finger

foot

feet

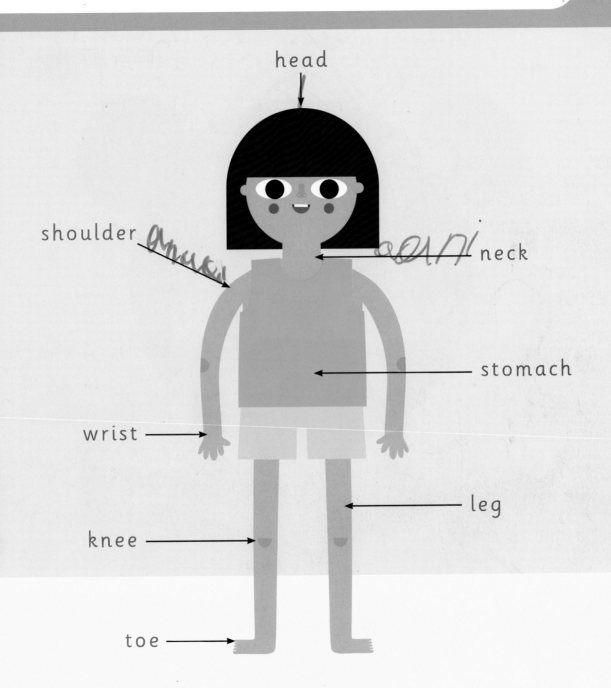

head

shoulder

neck

stomach

wrist

leg

knee

toe

My face

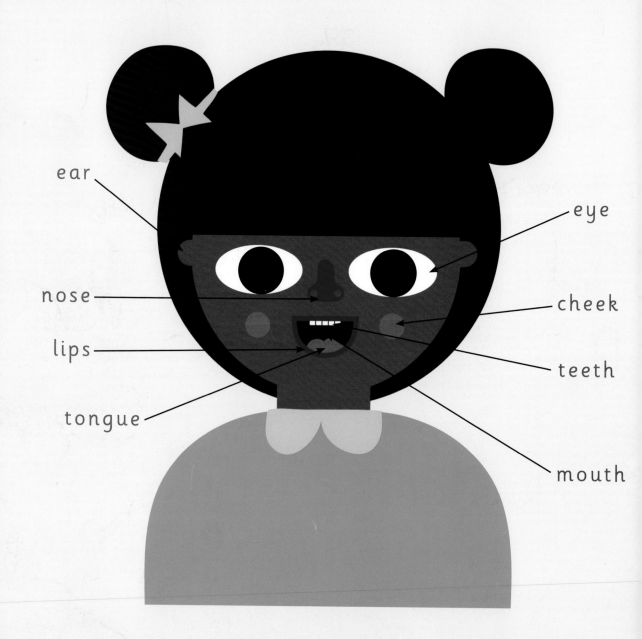

ear

eye

nose

cheek

lips

teeth

tongue

mouth

My senses

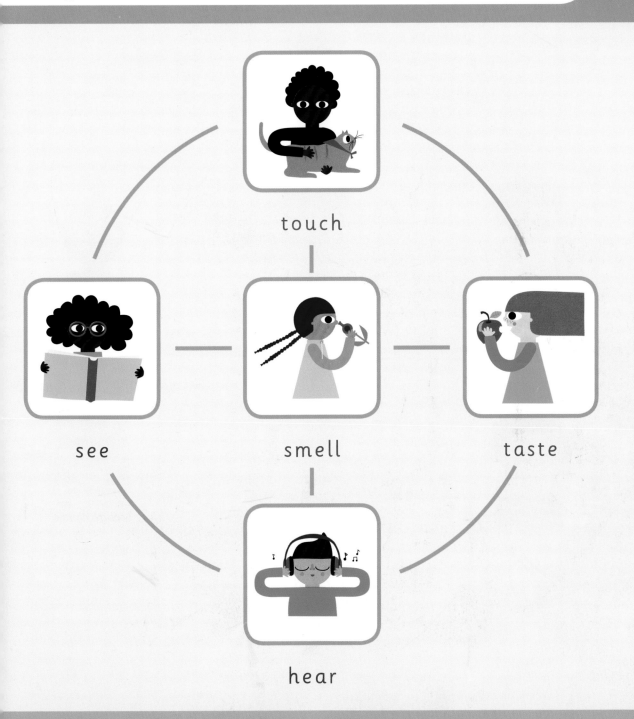

touch

see

smell

taste

hear

My hair

brown

ginger

grey

blond

dark

black

fair

What's your hair like?

short

beard

long

moustache

straight

curly

bald

My family

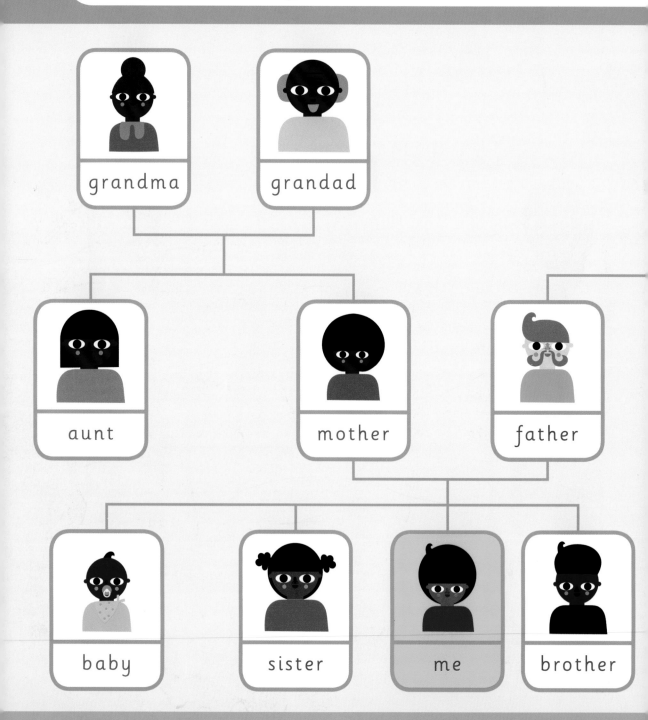

grandma

grandad

aunt

mother

father

baby

sister

me

brother

Who's in your family?

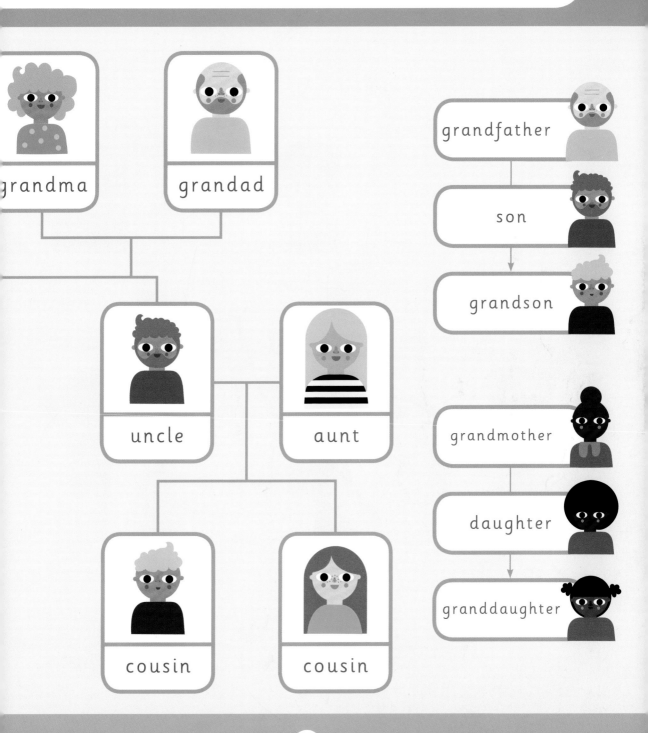

grandma

grandad

grandfather

son

grandson

uncle

aunt

grandmother

daughter

granddaughter

cousin

cousin

My feelings

happy

sad

angry

hungry

thirsty

tired

How are you feeling?

afraid

bored

excited

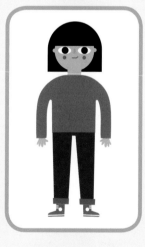

OK

good

great

My clothes

clothes

skirt

scarf

cardigan

dress

jumper

T-shirt

jacket

coat

What do you like to wear?

shorts

shoes

shirt

belt

glasses

trousers

gloves

socks

hat

My toys

ball

balloon

basketball

bike

boat

car

doll

football

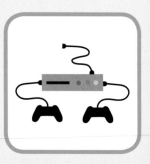

games console

Which toys do you like?

kite

helicopter

lorry

monster

plane

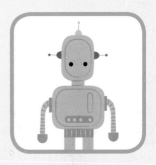

robot

teddy bear

train

video game

My hobbies

playing an instrument

playing sports

reading

drawing

painting

camping

playing outside

listening to music

singing

20

What do you like doing in your free time?

dancing

swimming

taking photos

watching television

walking

using the computer

cooking

playing games

gardening

My school bag

backpack

pen

pencil

rubber

pencil case

calculator

textbook

colouring pencils

scissors

What's in your school bag?

paper

sharpener

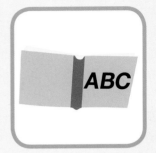

dictionary

notebook

sports kit

crayons

lunchbox

snack

juice

My pets

bird

mouse

cat

dog

puppy

guinea pig

hamster

horse

snake

Do you have any pets?

kitten

fish

tortoise

lizard

rabbit

rat

cage

hutch

fish bowl

Describing words

tall

short

old

young

friendly

funny

kind

sporty

brave

What are you like?

fat

thin

greedy

naughty

dirty

clean

big

small

lazy

My favourite food

bread

burger

chips

egg

fish

meat

ice cream

rice

sausage

What's your favourite food?

water

juice

breakfast

lemonade

milk

lunch

eat

drink

dinner

Fruit and vegetables

apple

banana

grapes

lemon

lime

mango

orange

pear

pineapple

What do you like to eat?

watermelon

beans

carrot

tomato

potatoes

onion

peas

fruit

vegetables

My home

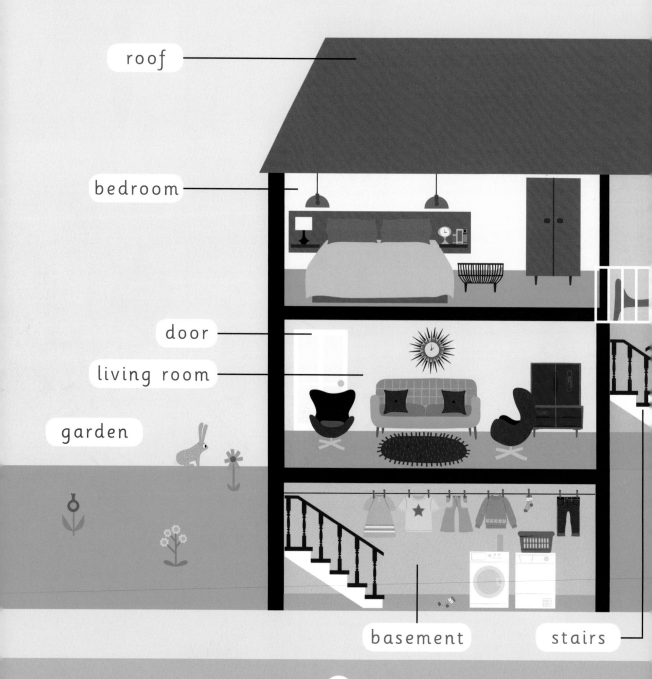

roof

bedroom

door

living room

garden

basement   stairs

What's inside your home?

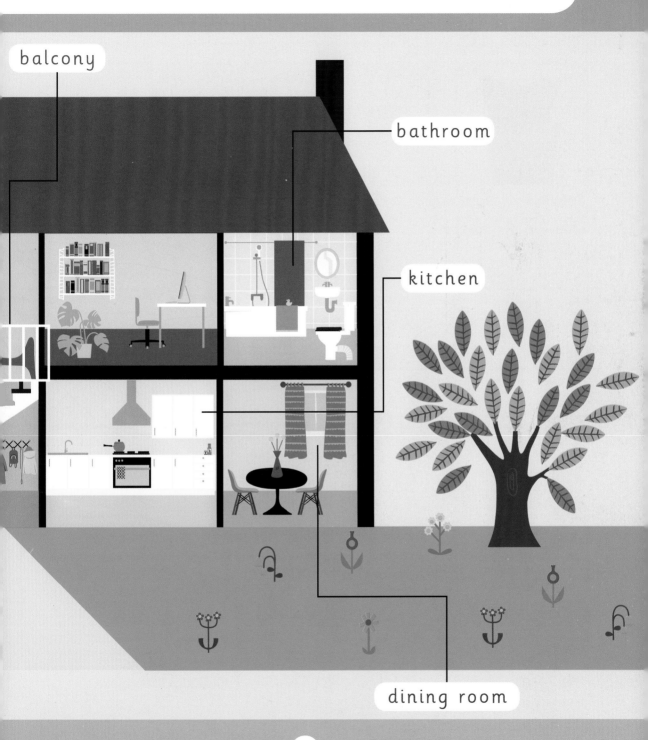

balcony

bathroom

kitchen

dining room

My living room

armchair

clock

sofa

lamp

television

book

bookcase

plant

window

What's in your living room?

table

painting

picture

phone

rug

mirror

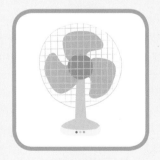

fan

tablet

cushion

In the kitchen

hob

oven

microwave

cupboard

radio

sink

fridge

fan

plate

What's in your kitchen?

fork

knife

bowl

spoon

mug

glass

cutlery

dining table

chair

My bedroom

bed

book shelf

clock

computer

desk

lamp

pillow

duvet

What's in your bedroom?

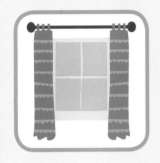

curtains

watch

toys

plant

photo

blanket

toybox

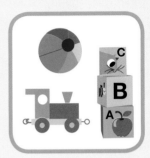

internet

The bathroom

bath

shower

mat

mirror

cupboard

toothbrush

towel

toothpaste

rubber duck

What do you find in your bathroom?

brush

comb

shelf

soap

toilet

toilet paper

shampoo

bubble bath

In the garden

sun

tree

flower

grass

leaf

sky

gate

wall

wheelbarrow

What's in the garden?

slide

swing

hedge

birds

watering can

vegetable patch

barbecue

lawnmower

greenhouse

My day

wake up

get up

brush my teeth

get dressed

have breakfast

go to school

have lunch

go home

do my homework

What will you do today?

have dinner

watch television

have a shower

wash my hair

read a story

go to bed

morning

afternoon

evening

Feeling unwell

headache

earache

toothache

stomach-ache

cold

cough

sore throat

cut

sneeze

What's the matter?

hurt

fever

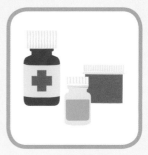

medicine

doctor

nurse

dentist

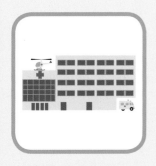

hospital

thermometer

ambulance